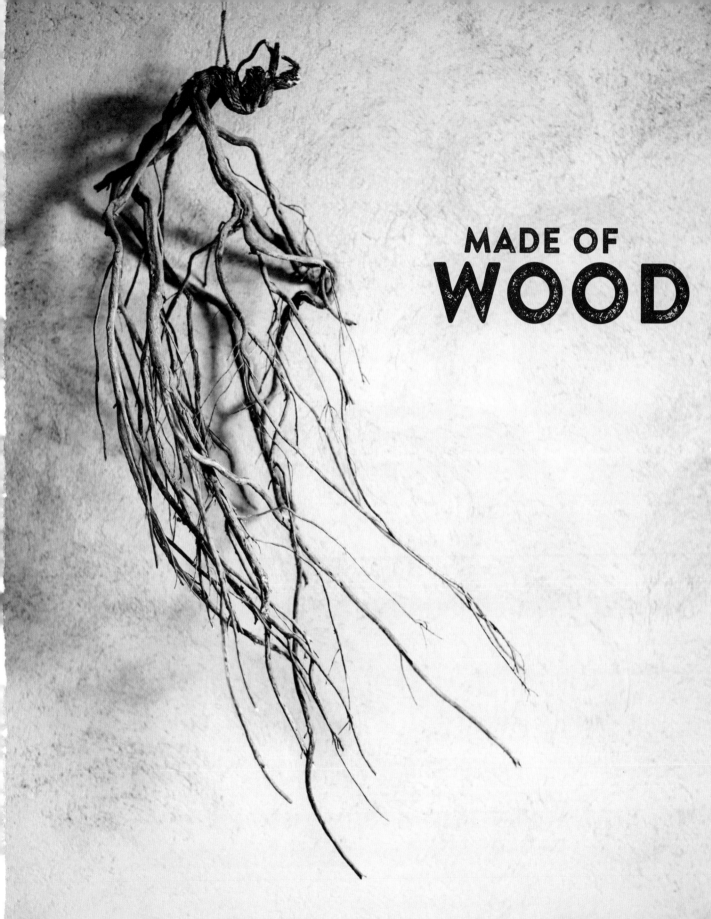

MADE OF
WOOD

MADE OF
WOOD
IN THE HOME

MARK & SALLY BAILEY

PHOTOGRAPHY BY DEBI TRELOAR

RYLAND PETERS & SMALL
LONDON • NEW YORK

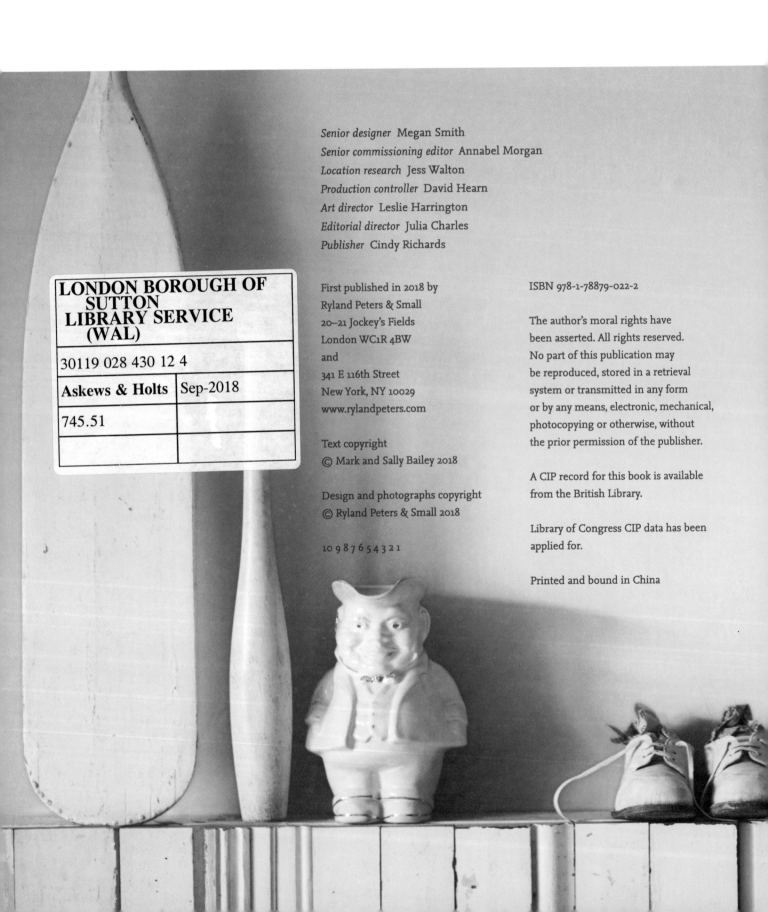

Senior designer Megan Smith
Senior commissioning editor Annabel Morgan
Location research Jess Walton
Production controller David Hearn
Art director Leslie Harrington
Editorial director Julia Charles
Publisher Cindy Richards

First published in 2018 by
Ryland Peters & Small
20–21 Jockey's Fields
London WC1R 4BW
and
341 E 116th Street
New York, NY 10029
www.rylandpeters.com

Text copyright
© Mark and Sally Bailey 2018

Design and photographs copyright
© Ryland Peters & Small 2018

10 9 8 7 6 5 4 3 2 1

ISBN 978-1-78879-022-2

A CIP record for this book is available
from the British Library.

Library of Congress CIP data has been
applied for.

Printed and bound in China

CONTENTS

INTRODUCTION

One damp Saturday afternoon, shortly after we moved into our home in the Welsh mountains, I was sitting at the table in my workroom pondering ideas for our next book. I thought of various titles, but kept going around in circles. I leaned back, put my feet on the table and looked up at the shelf. Staring back at me was a wooden hare given to us by our Japanese friend Yumiko.

The hare prompted one of those light-bulb moments. The new book would be about wood: homes made from it, homes full of wooden objects (both everyday and unusual) and how living with wood is a way to be close to nature while treasuring everyday craftsmanship.

Wood has been a constant in our lives for many decades. We have been working with recycled timber in our workshop for more than 30 years now and it forms a large part of what we sell in our store, from smooth, pale beech bowls, bread boards and utensils to the uncluttered lines of our stick-back chairs. These simple, unadorned objects we combine with country-made antique furniture, old factory workbenches and machinists' stools and chairs, with the emphasis on raw surfaces and the hand of the maker.

We have a weakness not for highly finished or polished timber objects but for those pieces that may have had ordinary origins yet are made extraordinary by their sculptural shapes, their industrial or agricultural history, or the way that they have been marked and scarred by age. The bread board scraped thin in the centre from

decades of cutting and slicing, or the shoe last that will never be used to form another piece of footwear, but lives on as a decorative object. Blackened by time, worn by use, bleached by the sun or smoothed by the sea, timber is a survivor.

Wooden buildings are sometimes associated with impermanence, but history doesn't bear that out: the Japanese temple Hōryū-ji is more than 1,400 years old, and there are many British examples of eccentrically crooked timber-framed barns and medieval manor houses. Wood is still a viable and sustainable way to construct a building, as many of the new homes in this book demonstrate, from contemporary mountain cabins to plywood-

lined houses. Aligned with the idea of sustainably built homes is a relatively new interest, the desire to live in a healthy environment unpolluted by chemicals, and here, too, timber comes into its own. Some of the homeowners in this book have furthered that cause by choosing to build with woods that do not require painting or treating. Instead, the timber slowly weathers to silvery grey tones and gets better with age.

As for the hare, he has become a mascot for this book. We have taken him with us to a few of the homes we photographed, and hidden him within the rooms; a secret to be discovered, and a symbol of wood's beauty, character and resilience.

OUR PHILOSOPHY

We've always believed that surrounding yourself with natural materials is a way to achieve a balanced and peaceful atmosphere in the home, and wood is the principal ingredient in that recipe for harmony. It conforms to almost every aspect of our wider philosophy: to be surrounded with hand-made objects; to embrace imperfection; and to celebrate humble, everyday things for their simple, sculptural beauty.

It is not difficult to create a home full of wood, not only because as a material it is so readily available, but that nearly all species of timber, all shapes and sizes of furniture and other objects, and all techniques to shape and decorate it, seem to produce an accord. This is especially true of old, weathered and patinated wood, whose matt surface and deep, mellow colours chime together so well.

Knowing this is helpful if you are trying to build up a collection of objects. Stick to one material, and you can barely go wrong. As your confidence grows, introduce something contrasting to bring the collection to life: a glossy piece of ceramic, a hand-made glass or something gilded or burnished to gleam out from among the matt timber. Seek out wooden items that have some personality, which could mean that they are old and worn, have an unusual shape, or that they retain some of the rawness of their natural state. Then let that personality take centre stage.

One easy way to introduce more wood into the home is to consciously choose it over plastic or metal for your most often-used tools and utensils, from bread boards and mixing spoons to scrubbing brushes, brooms and garden trowels. As well as being more pleasing to look at, wooden items are also much nicer to hold and touch, bringing tactile experience to daily rituals.

Generally speaking – opulent antiques aside – wood is an inexpensive material, and readily available second-hand. Sometimes it's free: several of the homes showcased in this book feature found objects, from driftwood to curiously shaped fragments abandoned in the corners of farmyards. Wood is resilient, and tends to look better with age, so it offers ample opportunity for its reinvention, which can be a satisfying aspect of making a home. Put your creativity to use by transforming a wooden piece of furniture with a wash of paint; scrubbing back a paint-laden door to reveal layers of colourful history; making shelving from old floorboards; or simply repurposing a usefully shaped object as a place to hang jewellery.

Houses full of wood have an embracing warmth about them. And even though the trees that created these interiors are no longer growing in the ground, that life and vitality is instilled in every knot, ring and grain. There is something very safe and comforting about being that close to nature.

WOODEN
ELEMENTS

SCULPTURAL

Wood is easily workable, a quality that means it can take on a multitude of forms. Describing wood as 'sculptural' perhaps implies a human hand at work, but we've found that some of the most interesting shapes can be fashioned entirely by nature, from driftwood whittled and pitted by the sea to wind-fallen kindling branches tied together.

Many everyday objects that nowadays might be made from plastic or metal were in the past made from wood, from games and toys to kitchen utensils. The wooden versions are often far more sculptural because they were made by hand rather than being cast or otherwise machine-made. Their individuality and imperfections make them prime items for display, especially if time has given them an attractive patina or human interaction has selectively worn them away. Spoons, chopping/cutting boards and bowls have excellent sculptural

properties, and if they can be taken down from the shelf and used, so much the better.

Similarly, industry has handed down many a curiously shaped tool or mould, from bobbins to hat blocks. Their curiosity is part of their appeal – not being able to put a finger on what they are tends to fire the imagination. Rhythm and repetition are important when it comes to arranging sculptural objects. Pieces might have a similar shape yet a different original purpose – an upward thrust or a smooth curve – but together they can create their own language.

Sculptural wooden objects don't have to be antiques. A single wooden spoon doesn't have great presence, yet a jar of them always looks appealing on a kitchen shelf; a bath brush hung on the wall, casting a long shadow from a side window, can be an artistic statement, if you choose it to be.

TAKING SHAPE
Curving wind-fallen branches are the raw material for Heidi Bjørnsdotter Thorvik's art (page 14). Ancient forms: curls of bark make delicate bracelets; a primitive-looking wooden figure in Heidi Bjørnsdotter Thorvik's home near Oslo was crafted by her father; a group of wonderfully three-dimensional, deeply scooped wooden spoons (page 15). A burr bowl and hollowed-out branch turned into a candlestick – functional objects in Marianne Vigtel Hølland's collection that are also close to nature (opposite). French wooden coin trays creatively present items of jewellery (above left). Turned wooden finials in a bowl at Jeanette Walther's rural home (above far left). A display in our home, backed by a collection of ware boards and old signage – each object is subtly tonally different to the next (left).

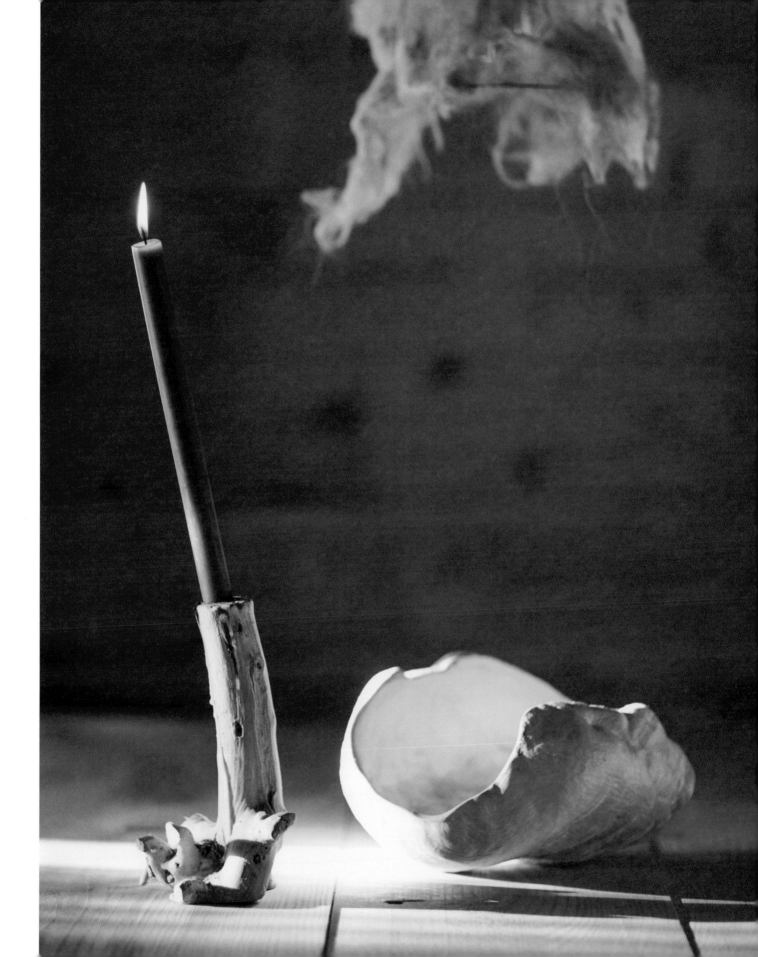

PATINATION OF THE PAST

Wooden objects reclaimed from the clothing industry such as hat blocks and glove moulds make some of the most intriguing sculptural objects – an eerie echo of a human hand or head (opposite). Old toys like skittle sets also make sculptural objects for display; nowadays, they would probably be made from plastic, which would not age or patinate as beautifully as wood. Alex Hoda bought these freestanding teak shelves from us to house tableware in the kitchen of his medieval home (above). The crooked grid of the beams provides a gentle contrast to the more regular structure of the shelving.

NATURAL

One of the recurring motifs in this book is the log stack: piles of wood, chopped into regularly sized chunks, all ready to feed the fire or stove. It's a nourishing sight, tapping into a primeval desire to feel secure in our homes – if there's enough wood to last the winter, survival is assured. But it's also the perfect demonstration of how wood in its natural (or nearly natural) state has compelling decorative appeal, too.

Sometimes nature needs only the gentlest of adjustments to transform something into a functional object – a gnarled branch used as a coat peg, or a cylindrical tree trunk thickly sliced to make a table or stool. These objects are powerful in their rawness, and some people find this soothing, making us feel as if the outside has come indoors to keep us company. Equally, a room entirely clad in natural timber has a calming, cocooning effect.

Timber comes in a variety of textures and hues, while different grains are the result not only of the species of tree but the way it has been cut and processed. Olive wood is prized for its tightly knotted, swirling grain, whereas pine's pale surface, punctuated by dark knots, lends itself to a simple, rustic aesthetic. Who would want to conceal such idiosyncrasies? By keeping the surface unadorned, these differences can be celebrated.

Paints, stains, oils and varnishes may be used to keep wood looking fresh, but if it is kept natural, it undergoes changes as it oxidizes. Many timbers get darker with age, achieving a blackness that cannot be replicated except by time, while others lose their tawny tones and lighten to grey and silver. Those timbers with a natural resilience, which can be used for the exterior of a building with no further maintenance needed, are truly remarkable.

IN THE RAW

Gnarled wooden plates; pale spoons stand out against a time-worn bowl; streamlined bent-plywood chairs (page 20). Untreated timber has an affinity with other natural materials, from sheepskin to knitted cushions (page 21). A decorative use of wood grain in a simple, modern kitchen (opposite). Displaying found and made wooden objects together highlights the differences in their colour and grain, with a giant shoe last on the floor offering a surreal touch (left); salt and pepper grinders and an elm bowl by Japanese craftsman Jiro Suda backlit against a window (above left); traditional cabins have a warm, cocooning effect thanks to their timber-clad walls (above).

TOUGHING IT OUT

Natural timber can be remarkably resilient, even in the harshest climates. Siberian larch has been used to clad this Icelandic house (above right): due to the trees' slow growth, the wood is rich in natural resin, which preserves it against rot and decay. Cedar is traditionally used for soaking tubs, because of its high impermeability to liquids (opposite). In this bathroom (above left), a wall of grainy reclaimed boards contrasts with the smooth tadelakt plaster finish of the wet room area.

TEXTURAL

Homes that use mainly natural materials to create something visually interesting often have texture as their defining characteristic. Tactile objects are doubly important, as they are not only pleasing to touch but to the eye, too. We would soon get bored if every surface was smooth and even, and the same would be true if every surface was roughly textured, so it becomes a case of learning to balance and create contrasts between different surface materials and finishes.

Wood offers texture in abundance and there is something quite meditative in running a hand over a piece of timber, tracing each knot and ring. And every species is different: take bark, and the rough, almost sharp texture of oak compared to silky and papery silver birch or dappled and patchy plane.

Timber creates fantastic textural interest as it ages, but the human hand can do so much more.

We collect Ethiopian furniture, which has the most amazing sculptural shapes and is also wonderful to handle, with every chisel mark visible and touchable. Such obviously hand-made objects provide a palpable link with their maker. We love to contrast raw and refined: an old floorboard stacked vertically next to a carved Rajasthani panel, or a turned table leg beside a rustic-looking bowl.

The texture of wood seems to work effortlessly with many other natural textures, such as slubby linen, soft wool, fluffy sheepskin and twisted rope. Together they create an air of calm and a feeling of honesty and authenticity. But a small amount of a contrasting texture can break that spell and provide a visual surprise: the polished copper pan on a wooden kitchen counter top; neat, angular brass brackets holding up aged timber shelves; or the gloss of a glazed ceramic plate on a dresser/hutch.

LAID BARE

Chopped, cracked and split, raw timber provides a variety of intriguing textural variation (page 26). Marianne Vigtel Hølland's hand-made coat hooks show layers of different surface finishes; the smooth-panelled walls juxtaposed with reclaimed wood and bare branches (page 27). A stone sink and distressed concrete create multiple layers of texture that subtly contrast with a timber-clad interior (opposite). Heavy, cracked and tarnished oak and elm studwork, infilled with pine boards (above left). Untreated timber has an affinity with other natural materials, from hemp to sheepskin (above right).

RAW AND REFINED
Smooth, knot-free wood is prized in many quarters – but grainy, knotted timber contains so much more personality and character in its surface detail (left). Regular and irregular; the strict symmetry of this table, with its turned legs, supports an asymmetrical display of pleasing wooden objects, including an Ethiopian stool and Rajasthani decorative panels (opposite.)

PAINTED

Historically, wood was painted principally to give it a layer of protection from the elements, but paint's decorative function is important, too. It can add a hit of enticing colour and pattern or create a blanket of calm when everything is painted a pale, soft white or calm grey. To us, there's not much sense in painting a piece of timber so thickly that you would never know what's underneath. A thin wash of paint brings out the texture of the grain, with the warmth of the natural wood colour still able to shine through.

Paint can also act as a unifying factor in a decorative scheme, and white or grey in particular bring an airy peacefulness to a space, as well as amplifying the daylight by reflecting it around the interior. Chalky, matt finishes are wonderful for their tonal variations and depth of colour, which introduce even more softness and serenity.

Of course, white never stays white for long, and the scrapes and marks of time can also be a compelling part of the story. We value the look of paint that has been worn away by time, whether on a well-loved old wooden toy or a scuffed floorboard, exposing the natural timber underneath. Distressed paintwork may not fit the original aim of providing a protective coating for bare wood , but it can be incredibly artful.

Some of the most exciting paintwork is achieved when successive generations of layers are removed from architectural features to reveal a beautifully complex pattern of colours and finishes. These vignettes on doors, window frames and skirting/base boards are like a journey into the past, revealing changing decorative trends and tastes. Stripping back the layers is a bit of a delicate operation – the challenge is knowing when to stop!

A BRUSH WITH WOOD

Furniture and architectural detailing takes on an ethereal, sculptural quality when painted in soft white and pale grey, and set against a white backdrop (pages 32 and 33, and above right). The scuffed surface of a chest of drawers is an equal match in terms of character to the crooked beams and ancient floorboards of a Herefordshire home (above left). Suffolk-based artist Jo Guinness uses paint to give a sense of unity to the disparate features of the kitchen in her guest annexe (opposite), from the beams to the cabinetry – the overall effect is a patchwork of black, white and grey, as well-proportioned and balanced as a painting itself. Pieces of traditional painted furniture contrast with rough hewn planks and a wall of chopped logs at Antonio Bembo and Anda Hobai's Romanian hunting lodge (overleaf).

RECYCLED

Wood's longevity and malleability mean it can go through many lifetimes of use, changing its function as it goes. You can mend with it, whittle it away to create something else or, if it has an interesting enough shape or texture, simply appreciate it as a decorative object. Old wood has so much character and often looks better with age, it's no wonder that people would rather find a way to reuse it than discard it.

This book is full of examples of wooden objects that have been recycled. Sometimes, not too much reinvention is required: old floorboards used to clad walls or make headboards and doors; or raw branches strung together to create a place to hang a coat. But in other cases, the transformation is a little more imaginative: chairs stripped down to their frames to become sculptural objects, revealing the skeletal beauty of the craftsmanship behind

them, or a stringer from a staircase salvaged and repurposed as a decorative cornice/crown molding.

Many wooden objects in our home have an industrial or agricultural past, and, no longer required for the job, have become curiosities that are not just interesting to look at but also tell a story. They are familiar yet unfamiliar, and that is all part of the appeal. Old wooden mill bobbins and plumbers' beads (used to flare lead pipework) make interesting lights when strung together, turning obsolete objects into functional ones again.

Recycling is, of course, also a way to be less wasteful, a subject that should resonate with everyone, and by using old timber instead of new, there are no concerns about sustainable sourcing. Wood is a material that lowers carbon emissions, and making sure that it has as long a life as possible is one more argument for its use.

SECOND TIME AROUND

Elegant forms: old wooden objects given a new life
for use in the home (pages 38 and 39). A configuration
of vertically stacked thick floorboards and decorative
carved panels in our Welsh farmhouse (above). Old
exercise pins look like slender figures when 'dressed'
with bracelets (right). Touches of brass enliven a group
of recycled boards and a hat block (above right). An
oak Edwardian swivel chair and trestle table bought
from a local village hall (opposite). Jo Guinness's
Suffolk studio is full of furniture that she has bought
and then painted or reupholstered; the graphic cornice/
crown molding running round the room was once
the stringer board of a staircase (overleaf).

WOODEN
STORIES

CABIN FEVER

Marianne Vigtel Hølland works under the name Slow Design Studio, and her ethos is as much a part of her life as it is her work. Her weekend house, a mountain retreat near Lillehammer, north of Oslo, is a tribute to her ability to create a soothing home that's all about decelerating from the pace of city life while showcasing her talents as a maker.

The house has two parts, an old traditional Norwegian log cabin and a modern extension designed by Marianne's sister, an architect, and built by Marianne and her husband. When the couple bought the cabin a decade ago, it was small and suited their young family well enough, but had no running water or road access – they had to ski down from the road to reach it. When the local council sold off some neighbouring land, the whole area was upgraded, and with water and a paved road in place, it became possible to extend.

Although the extension has modern features such as underfloor heating and picture windows that open up the space to some incredible views, the couple wanted to respect the building's origins as a humble cabin as well as the surrounding landscape and local architectural vernacular. The new addition takes its inspiration from traditional mountain barns, which farmers would live in during the summer months while watching over their livestock. Its exterior is constructed from the heartwood of Norwegian pine – the hardest and most durable part of the wood – with aspen for the interior cladding, which has been treated with iron oxide to ebonize it, changing its colour to a warm grey. A polished concrete floor bounces the clear mountain light around the spacious rooms.

Many features, including the kitchen, have been made from reclaimed barn wood. A century old, this knotted and weathered timber is rough and rustic, a contrast to industrial elements such as the bare-bulb pendant lights hanging over the kitchen island, and the concrete floor. "It felt right to bring some old elements into the new part of the cabin," says Marianne. In the old cabin, a long stretch of built-in seating has been filled with sheepskins and blankets, a feature that has been replicated in the extension. There are also two identical dining tables, one in the old cabin and one in the new living space; made from ash with raw steel legs fabricated by a local blacksmith, they can be put together when necessary to seat guests.

Besides the use of local timber, many other elements anchor the interiors in Norwegian culture, from the reclaimed military blanket with *Norge* emblazoned across it, to the wool that Marianne used to make lamps and chair covers and that comes from an ancient breed of sheep, the Old Norwegian Spælsau. Wool is very much Marianne's design medium: she's a prolific self-taught freestyle knitter and creates wool installations. The house contains many examples of her skill, including unexpected objects such as the pendant over one of the dining tables, made from wool that she has felted into the shape of a lampshade.

Hardly anything in the house has been bought new. As well as making as much as she could herself, Marianne sourced furniture and decorative objects from flea markets and thrift shops, seeking out mid-century furniture, wooden candlesticks and carved burr bowls. "I prefer natural materials and like to balance different kinds of materials: new and old, soft and hard, light and heavy," says Marianne. "It is important to me to surround myself with things that have a story."

The hand-made elements in the house epitomize Marianne's 'slow design' philosophy, and, together with the beautiful views, they give the interior an innate calmness. Yes, hand-made takes more time, but it is also about mindfulness, and finding pleasure in the act of making, as well as being able to enjoy the captivating results.

WEATHERED WOOD

Marianne has used century-old reclaimed Norwegian barn wood to make her kitchen (opposite). The planks have weathered to a silvery grey, but the edges have been rubbed back to reveal the true colour of the wood (above). The sink and work surfaces have been cast in a silky smooth concrete. Above the sink is a brass wall-mounted Vola tap/faucet (above left).

IN THE GROOVE

The polished concrete floor in the kitchen area has underfloor heating and an open fireplace has been installed to cosy up this area (above). Sheepskins add warmth and texture throughout (above and right). All the boarded ceilings and walls in the cabin have been clad in aspen – a soft white wood often associated with the production of paper and matches. The timber has been treated with iron oxide, which ebonizes the wood, turning it a rich honey colour in the process (opposite and overleaf).

PANORAMIC PLEASURES

With far-reaching views across the valley, the large window openings are an important feature of the design of the cabin; Marianne's idea being that wherever you are in the building you feel part of the landscape (above, opposite and overleaf). Running the full width of the cabin is a wooden bench seat with storage drawers underneath (opposite). The seat is layered up with thick, tactile blankets and sheepskins, as well as knitted and knotted cushions made by Marianne (above right).

WELSH FARMHOUSE

Maesgwyn is our bolthole deep in the Welsh mountains. A remote 18th-century farmhouse surrounded by sheep and skylarks, it overlooks the Black Mountains and the Brecon Beacons National Park, and we fell in love with its location and unrivalled views.

We were not lucky enough to have bought a house that could simply be stripped back to reveal its original features, so we have recreated these using reclaimed materials found on our travels. Most of the upper floors were chipboard and we replaced these with antique oak boards. In the bedroom, bathroom and studio, we reinstated the oak and elm studwork walls using old pine floorboards to infill; the old nail-holes and the gaps between each board let in lovely slivers of light. Displaying collections of wooden objects such as folding rulers on these walls adds further to the textural effect, whereas elsewhere more colourful objects like books and paintings stand out against their woody background.

The house's renovation saw the internal walls taken back to bare stone before a new, highly insulated timber skin was added on top and then lime plastered. Underfloor heating lies beneath the ground concrete floor. Making the fabric of the house as energy efficient as possible was a priority; it meant we could install a renewable energy source (a ground-source heat pump, which harnesses natural heat from underground), taking us well on our way to our goal of being completely off-grid. An adjacent stone barn acts as a plant room for the heat pump and water filtration system; fully renovating the barn is our next project.

The ground floor is open plan, with a wet room and a bedroom leading off the kitchen at one end of the house. This was once the pigsty and log store. Reclaimed and reused objects are a recurring theme, especially in the kitchen. The island was built in our workshop from leftover floorboards and sits on steel legs, with a thick, honed black granite worktop to add a heavier contrasting finish. An old French bakery table has been turned into a sink stand to house the ceramic farmhouse sink, with an old gun cupboard used as a store for herbs and spices. The kitchen table, with its indestructible black linoleum surface, came from a works canteen. The shelves behind it are made from elm beams, with brackets of folded brass designed by Mark – a golden gleam that radiates out from the chalky white walls and raw wood. These shelves are packed with our favourite studio pottery, which we use daily. The black sheep that hangs above the sofa was made from old stained floorboards. It was based on an original metal sign that hung at an agricultural merchants in Hay-on-Wye.

The bedroom's high ceilings allowed us to create a playful feature for our grandchildren: an old jute hammock hangs from the purlins, with a tall wooden ladder leading up to it. We made the

oak bed and headboard from massive thick floorboards. These originally came from a bonded warehouse in Wales; we used the reverse side of the boards, with their deep-cut marks, as we felt that they were more interesting (but less comfortable).

With the exception of a few textiles, ceramics, books and artwork, the whole house has a pared-down palette of chalky white walls, grey concrete floors and an abundance of raw wood throughout. Every time we arrive, we feel the calmness of the space and the surroundings wash over us. It feels like a world away from our hectic lives with only the sound of bleating sheep in the background.

OPEN HOUSE

An open-plan layout is unexpected in an 18th-century building, but it brings as much space and light as possible to the ground floor, with an open staircase creating a natural demarcation between living spaces. In the kitchen area, the sink stand was once a French bakery table (above left and right). The island was made in our workshop from reclaimed floorboards with a top of honed black granite (opposite).

COMFORT FARM

The renovation work saw a new layer of insulation added to the walls, with underfloor heating installed beneath the concrete floors (opposite). These measures, plus the regular use of more conventional heating methods in the form of the original cooking range, ensure that the farmhouse is incredibly warm and snug during the winter months. The wooden table next to the range is an old French wine table. We already owned a metal version of this sheep (above), and loved it so much that we decided to make another from old timber floorboards. It watches over a linen-covered Baileys Loft Sofa.

SLEEPING BEAUTY

The ground-floor bedroom is a simple, tranquil space, with timber-clad half-height walls acting as a bed headboard (above left). The upstairs bedroom, meanwhile, has a headboard made from thick reclaimed floorboards with their cut undersides facing outwards for visual interest (above right). Taking advantage of the upstairs bedroom's open eaves and high ceilings, a hammock has been hung from the purlins, accessed by a wooden ladder that has been whitewashed to create a graduated effect (opposite). The house had chipboard floors upstairs when we bought it – now, wide-plank antique oak floorboards have completely transformed the character of the space.

CLEAN LIVING

In the wet room, a leaning ware board stores bathing essentials, thanks to the addition of ceramic soap dishes (opposite). The wooden jugs are Hungarian – the delicate pattern is burned into the surface. Mark recycled driftwood to make a handle for a bath brush (above left and above). The white ceramic basin contrasts with a dark oak plank laid across it (left), and an old Spanish anvil (above) has also found a home here.

OAK AND ELM

An abstract patterned skirt in shades of tan and ochre is silhouetted against a ledge and brace door (left). We rebuilt the oak and elm studwork walls, using pine floorboards to fill the gaps. The shelf holds an unframed painting by Arthur Neal, alongside a row of wooden exercise pins, which has been made even more visually arresting with stacked-up bracelets (below). The chromatic intensity of indigo-dyed fabrics works particularly well with aged wood (opposite).

WONDER WALLS

Interior designer Jeanette Walther has peeled back the layers of her 300-year-old house to reveal some hidden gems. Off came half a dozen layers of wallpaper, up came the old carpets and down came a thick mantle of ivy that concealed the exterior to uncover treasures that had lain in wait all along. The cherry red and cream antique ceramic tiles in the kitchen, for example, were buried under layers of other tiles that had to be very carefully chipped away, but a little damage is OK, too – it all helps to tell the story.

The former coach house is in the small village of Sprockhövel-Hasslinghausen on the outskirts of Wuppertal in western Germany, and was a complete mess when Jeanette and her husband Stefan bought the place a decade ago. Now restored, it is not merely a demonstration of Jeanette's talent for bringing together rough, raw and textured objects to create a warmly lived-in feel, but also a place that anyone who passes by can experience. She runs her design business from the vaulted basement, while the ground floor is open to the public and everything on show there is for sale. Jeanette and her family live upstairs, so there is a sense of privacy despite the fact that half the house is in effect a shop floor.

A 3m/10ft-high front door announces the house's grandeur – back in the day when this was a coach house, several families would have lived here. The ground floor contains several living

spaces as well as a working kitchen, all full of intriguing objects artfully displayed.

Jeanette called on Stefan's carpentry skills in several areas of the house. He created the antique barn wood panels that cover one of the chimney breasts and also built the kitchen, which is made from reclaimed wood. The dishwasher has been concealed behind a leather panel; a clever way of hiding a modern convenience that would have jarred with the rest of the room.

Simple, rustic furniture and a soothing palette of greys and blues create a warm, comforting atmosphere here. There is an absence of shiny materials – most of the metal is dull and aged, with the exception of the gleaming tap/faucet and cooker – making the whole house a harmonious interplay of matt surfaces. Textural interest dominates, from the little timber birdhouses to the woven rugs and knitted cushions.

Pattern is mostly absent, but not colour; some of the walls are painted muted pink or mineral blue, with displays of wooden objects creating compelling silhouettes in front of them. A petrol blue dresser/hutch in the kitchen houses old wooden boards and a collection of ceramics.

Weathered and patinated materials are a dominant theme in the house, from the acid-treated metal panels that make up the kitchen splashback to the Chinese and Nepalese antiques. Often, a closer look is needed before it's clear

ATMOSPHERIC CONDITIONS

Jeanette's home doubles as her
place of work. It is a scene of
much change and experimentation,
yet still manages to feel calm and
atmospheric. In the living room,
the sculptural lamp on the windowsill
is beautifully outlined against the
daylight, and the pendant lamp,
with its multiple metal discs, provides
another intriguing silhouette
(opposite). Behind a work area is
a canvas painted by Jeanette (right).

what an item is – are those discs forming the
components of a pendant light wooden or metal?
An unframed panel that hangs on the wall behind
the work area is the colour of verdigris and at first
glance could easily be mistaken for dulled copper,
but it is actually a piece of heavy painted canvas.
Although the panel may look antique, Jeanette
made it herself. These visual tricks add to the
sense of intrigue in this house.

Outside there is a large garden, which has also
required significant restoration, and a fountain
that once served the coach house.

The beauty of living somewhere that doubles
as a retail space is that the interior is always in a
state of flux, one object leaving only to be replaced
by another. This constant change satisfies
Jeanette's urge for creative experimentation while
moving on the house's 300-year history apace.

AN AIR OF CALM

Jeanette mixes new furniture, such as the metal-legged coffee table (opposite), with old, like the drawer-fronted table with its bench seating behind (above right). It all fits together because of her skill at mirroring textures and surfaces, which are almost universally unpolished and matt. This approach seems to lay a blanket of calm over everything. A pair of metal bowls picks up the same soft burnished finish and curving shape of the pendant lamp that hangs above; the linen-covered sofas echo the textiles that have been used for the curtains. A few more decorative, textured objects, selectively chosen, have been included to catch the eye, such as a knitted cushion (above left) or a textile wall-hanging.

ROUGHLY RUSTIC
Squares of patinated metal serve as a splashback behind the kitchen sink; a rustic–industrial take on traditional tiling (opposite). The gleaming chrome tap/ faucet stands out as the only shiny surface among the dulled metal, wood, ceramic and concrete. The original floor tiles were buried under several layers of flooring and had to be carefully uncovered (right).

A BALANCE OF COLOUR

The muted palette has been carefully chosen to act as a subtle backdrop to each room, with scuffed or matt finishes providing an extra layer of texture. A dresser/hutch (above) holds ceramics and wooden bowls (opposite above left); green-grey walls contrast with the warmer-toned floorboards (opposite above right); while blues and greens give storage baskets and wooden maquettes a strong outline (opposite below right). At first glance, a painted canvas panel looks like patinated copper (opposite below left).

SUFFOLK FARMHOUSE

Jo Guinness lives not far from the coast in a rural area of Suffolk known locally as The Saints, full of quiet lanes and clusters of villages with medieval churches. When we arrived, Jo had just fed her chickens and welcomed us into her 300-year-old Dutch-style gabled farmhouse.

Jo trained as an artist in London before making a move to the Suffolk countryside. "The big skies and quality of light are what drew me to this area," says Jo. Since moving here over a decade ago, she feels rooted to this part of the world. "I've become part of a community of artisans, artists and musicians who were all drawn here for similar reasons. I just knew that it was here I wanted to be."

The farmhouse is heavily beamed with a reclaimed brick floor, panelled walls, exposed boarded ceilings and two winding staircases. Everything has been given Jo's signature Scandinavian-style paint finish: a wash of subtle pale grey that is then rubbed, scrubbed and scraped back to give a worn, layered effect.

Jo's favourite place to sit in the house is in the kitchen next to the cream-coloured Aga range cooker with her two dogs. Over the Aga is a huge oak lintel flanked by two built-in cupboards that have been given Jo's washed paint finish. Above to the right hangs one of Jo's jug paintings and below it another jug painting, this one by Jo's friend Claire Halsey. Further along the wall, Jo's wide ceramic sink is sat on two columns of painted bricks below

a pair of wall-mounted brass bib taps/faucets. Between the sink and the Aga, Jo has used freestanding furniture of differing heights, including a corner cupboard topped with olive oils and spices above which hang more paintings. The overall effect is of a well-equipped, slightly bohemian kitchen with everything close to hand. Jo's bathroom leads straight off the kitchen. Here, a cast-iron roll-top bathtub has been cleverly framed with a patchwork of limewashed horizontal floorboards, and a painted cabinet is propped precariously on the rim of the tub.

At each end of the house is a painted oak winding staircase that Jo has carpeted using coarse Hungarian striped hemp. The stairs lead up to three interconnecting bedrooms with original wattle and daub walls. One of these has been cleverly exposed to show how the wall was constructed, also letting extra light into this room. A brass and iron bed fits snugly into the alcove. All the bedrooms have painted floors layered with antique rugs, giving them a light and airy feel.

Across the yard in the paddock stand two wooden stables that were formerly part of a horse sanctuary and had fallen out of use. With the help of local builders, Jo has converted these stables into a light-filled studio and workshop where she works on her numerous painting and crafting projects. Jo buys many pieces of furniture in need of repair from the local Diss Auction Rooms. "It doesn't

Two jug paintings (the top one by Jo)
flank the Aga in the main kitchen
(left); Jo's quiet style of painting is
a good complement to the rough
painted brickwork and an ancient
lintel. A patchwork of fabrics make
up a diaphanous curtain (opposite
above left), while the winding stair
is carpeted in coarse hemp (opposite
above right). An old radiator occupies
one of the huge fireplaces (opposite
below right). Jo's signature finish
of subtle grey paint, washed and
scrubbed back, gives the house
a sense of unity – here it's used on
an old door that acts as a splashback
(opposite below left).

matter where it's come from originally, as long
as the shape is good. I'll strip it right back to its
workings and start again from there." Jo's studio
is so well equipped that she need not leave – after
a hard day's work she can take a long, luxurious
bath and throw herself onto the sofa.

The bathroom in the studio, which is hidden
behind a pair of painted French shutters, is a
real statement. The monolithic stone bathtub had

previously been used as a horse trough and took
six men to install, while the rusty corrugated-iron
panel used as a splashback was found in a ditch
nearby. Over the tub hangs a modern shower with
the rose concealed by an upturned dolly tub.

Throughout her home and studio, Jo's ingenuity
in using recycled materials is evident – she has
used a salvaged wooden stair string as a cornice/
crown molding running around the studio.

REFLECTIONS OF LIGHT

Whitewashing wood brings out an ethereal quality – on this door, the drip marks have been left to dry, giving it an even more painterly look, and the pale colour of the walls and furniture reflects the beautiful Suffolk light (opposite). Jo has an eye for chairs with unusual silhouettes, which she paints to harmonize with their surroundings (above left); here there is a lovely tonal play between the various matt surfaces on the walls, the mirror and the chair. A wall of reclaimed boards, each scuffed, marked and painted in a unique way, creates a focal point in the bathroom (above right). An old corner cupboard balances on the side to store the practical necessities for bathing.

LIVE/WORK SPACE

Jo converted the old stables into a workshop and studio for herself, but the space is well-appointed enough to act as guest accommodation, with a kitchen, dining space, bathroom and bedroom (previous spread and opposite). In the kitchen, a salvaged wooden stair string has been reinvented as a cornice/ crown molding running around the room, a tribute to Jo's creative ingenuity (above right). By the window hangs a rack of tools used for painting and making (above left).

BLACK & WHITE
HOUSE

Hollyhocks sits on the banks of the River Arrow among ancient apple and cider orchards in the village of Eardisland in north Herefordshire. This medieval half-timbered longhouse lies among neighbouring black and white houses dating from the 16th and 17th centuries. These buildings were traditionally built from green (unseasoned) oak and panels infilled with woven wooden lathes that were covered with lime plaster, then painted with limewash and tinted with natural pigments. Painting the panels white and the beams black using Stockholm tar is a relatively recent idea – before this, the timbers were left unpainted to weather naturally.

Hollyhocks is a house that embraces its long history. There are 12 red roses painted on one of the beams of the great hall, recording that 12 knights slept here the night before they headed off to meet their fate in the Wars of the Roses at the battle of Mortimer's Cross in 1461.

The house, parts of which date from the late 14th century, had been in Alex Hoda's family for some years, and when his grandmother passed it down to him, it was time to renovate. Alex and his wife Danielle used a local saw mill to cut the oak needed to repair some of the beams and the floors were lifted for new wiring and plumbing to be installed. The natural materials and neutral palette make for a calm and unified feel.

The Great Hall – once a tithe barn – is now an open-plan kitchen-dining-living space, with a freestanding concrete-wrapped kitchen island that contains all the necessary storage and appliances. Alex didn't want to have kitchen cabinets attached to the beams, preferring to keep a sense of the space as a barn, so the kitchen is as separate and contemporary-looking as possible. It's a big room, so the island acts as both a focal point and a means of dividing up the space. The same line of thought lay behind the choice of the large industrial-style metal pendant lights: as these are an anachronistic modern addition, why not go for something completely contrasting and defiantly non-domestic? This room also has a spectacular parquet floor that was laid in the 1920s by the Twinings family (owners of the eponymous tea company) on the occasion of their daughter's wedding. There are further references to this connection in some of the bedrooms, where tea chests are used as bedside tables/night stands.

When it came to choosing antique and reclaimed furniture and fittings, Alex and Danielle applied the same sensibility as they had to the building. In the flagstoned hallway hangs an old wooden sledge, and a butter churn acts as an umbrella stand. One of the bed headboards is a deconstructed Afghan chest, while the bathroom mirror was once a sash window. A church pew

looks perfectly at home in the kitchen, providing a place to perch and chat while someone is cooking. A row of Romanian flax combs, originally used to untangle the plant's fibres to prepare them for spinning, is mounted on the wall here. Seeing all the linen in the room, Alex decided he wanted something on the wall that would reflect the origins of the fabric itself – and, of course, these wooden combs sit very happily in what was once a barn.

It's no coincidence that these objects are all made from wood – their strong shapes and rich patination create a feeling of unity with the structure of the house, so there's always a dialogue between the architecture and the interior spaces.

From the outside, the half-timbered house, with its bulges and blackened, crooked beams, is as chocolate-box perfect as anyone could wish for. In the garden, there is one last piece of extraordinary local history, a thatched cider barn believed to be the last of its kind in Herefordshire.

LATHE AND PLASTER
Half-timbered, with lathe and plaster walls, Hollyhocks is a traditional medieval longhouse (previous spread and opposite). The neutral palette gives the interior a sense of timeless tranquillity (above left and right). In the open-plan kitchen, a Baileys Loft Sofa offers a place to relax (opposite).

THE GREAT HALL

There are 12 red roses painted on one of the ancient beams of the great hall (left and opposite). Legend has it that this is where 12 knights slept before they headed off to meet their fate at the battle of Mortimer's Cross in 1461, during the Wars of the Roses.

TRANQUIL BATHING

The atmospheric bathroom has crooked beams, sloping ceilings and uneven wooden floors (above). Alex and Danielle chose a freestanding cast-iron roll-top bathtub, along with a wall-mounted trough sink and a bathroom mirror made from an old sash window (opposite above left and right). The walls have been boarded in practical tongue and groove. In one of the bedrooms, the headboard is made from a deconstructed Afghan chest (opposite below right). The bedside table/night stand is an old tea chest, a reference to the Twinings family of Twinings Tea, who once owned the house.

UNDER THE THATCH
In the orchard stands one of Herefordshire's last-remaining cider barns, complete with all its horse-drawn stone workings.

SUPERNATURAL

Artist Heidi Bjørnsdotter Thorvik's childhood was spent in the fjords and forests of Norway, and this rural upbringing has had a deep and lasting effect on her and her work. Her father is a skilled woodworker who restores traditional buildings, while her grandmother was a weaver and seamstress. These familial threads come together in her art, which uses both textiles and foraged natural materials such as driftwood and plants.

Although Heidi now lives with her husband on the outskirts of Oslo, she has not quite left the forest behind. Their 1920s house may be only 20 minutes from the centre of the city, but it's surrounded by woodland. The couple bought the house five years ago, attracted partly by the work that the previous owner had done to the place – the roof in the open-plan living space had been opened up to the rafters, creating a cavernous room dominated by beautiful exposed timber beams. There is also a woodworking studio full of the hand tools that Heidi uses in her work. The making also spills out elsewhere in the house, for example in the *oppstadveven* (upright weaving loom) she has made to a very ancient design, its ghostly white driftwood branches giving it an eerie presence.

Heidi works under the name Vølt, a word derived from *vøle*, meaning 'to repair' in her native dialect. Her philosophy is to find the beauty in the old, the worn and the discarded, and to give these objects new life through craftsmanship. This ethos is repeatedly shown in her house, where the coat hooks are old nails hammered into a board, and slices of tree branch become buttons on a cushion. She is endlessly creative: driftwood is made into jewellery or coat hangers; bark is turned into a bracelet; tree stumps make monolithic stools or side tables. Her work makes you look anew at every abandoned object, and wonder how it could be given a new lease of life.

There's an ethical, anti-consumerist side to this philosophy, especially when the raw materials are foraged or found. Heidi sources driftwood from the lakes near her childhood home, and finds storm-fallen branches in the forest that surrounds her house. Worn, lived-in materials, from natural sheep's wool to rusted metal, are her preference, for the sense of history and informality that they bring. Wood is special to Heidi, though, because it is "the material that is as close to nature as you can get", and for its versatility. It's also easy to repair a wooden object, or use wood to repair another object, so it fits with her 'make do and mend' ethos.

"We like a calm atmosphere. Not too much stuff, not too much mess," is how she describes her style at home. But not everything here is natural and imperfect. A cement Loop chair by Swiss modernist designer Willy Guhl sits next to the stove in the kitchen, its smooth, sinuous curves offering a contrast to the log store that is its backdrop. Oversized Edison bulbs and metal concertina wall lights bring an industrial edge, and there is also lots of comfortable mid-century furniture.

The pieces that are the most special to Heidi have a story to tell, and they are all made from wood. A cabinet in the workroom was a wedding gift, made by her father from 200-year-old wood from an old cottage he had been restoring. She also has a loom that belonged to her grandmother – Heidi's aunt gave it to her, knowing how close the bond had been between grandmother and granddaughter. A beautifully worn wooden workbench in her studio was a present from her husband, who searched high and low to find the right one for her. "It's really important that I use it," she says of the workbench. "I don't want tools for decoration. I find it really satisfying to use them."

COMPOSED CORNERS

A work in progress hangs from the wall, its hand-made needles and chunky ball of natural wool both a part of the balanced composition, with rusty nail sculptures on the table (above left). The smooth curves of a cement chair by Swiss designer Willy Guhl sit in front of the log store, a little tree-trunk table perched beside it (above right). Rustic materials are contrasted with elegant mid-century furniture (opposite). A view from the mezzanine level reveals the open-plan living and eating space (overleaf).

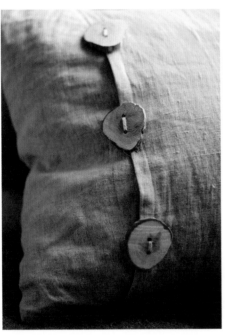

CLOSE TO NATURE

Reuse and reinvention are at the heart of Heidi's philosophy – like the tree-branch buttons that she sewed onto a cushion while we were visiting (above left). In the bathroom, the right angles of a wooden storage cabinet are beautifully offset by the gently curving branch that leans against it (above right). A daybed is strewn with large cushions to provide an inviting space to unwind, with a shaggy sheepskin rug to soften and warm the hard flooring, and a Jieldé floor light, a French industrial design classic dating back to the 1950s, to read by (opposite).

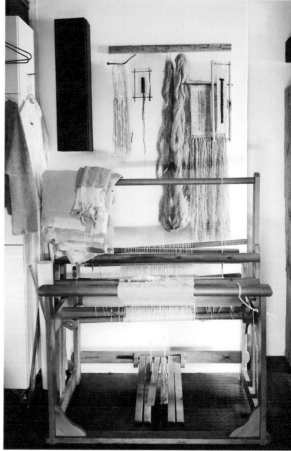

WOVEN AND WOODEN

Weaving and woodworking are in Heidi's blood, and evidence of both appear everywhere in her home and the workshop. The ghostly driftwood weighted loom, an *oppstadveven*, was made to an ancient design (opposite), while its more modern equivalent once belonged to Heidi's grandmother (right). The wooden open cabinet is one of Heidi's most treasured belongings. A wedding present made by her father from timber reclaimed from an old cabin he was restoring, it's used for storing antique linen remnants (above right). In the workshop, neatly stacked and sorted timber, including driftwood foraged from the lakeland countryside, awaits a new life (above).

THE CHICKENSHED

With a hillside location in the Wye Valley looking towards the Black Mountains' Sugar Loaf peak, the view is everything at The Chickenshed. Yet, as the name suggests, its rural location was once enjoyed only by poultry. Thankfully, such an injustice has now been righted, and where there was once a dilapidated barn for raising chicks now sits a secluded holiday let that offers simple, uncluttered comfort to its visitors.

Owner Sue Peacock and her husband Nick, who live on a nearby farm, bought the property at auction, not only because they saw the potential of the site, but also because it came with planning permission for a holiday home designed by architects Martin Hall and Kelly Bednarczyk, with whom the couple had a history – the practice had already worked on an extension to their own home. The footprint of the new building is exactly the same as the old shed, but it would be a stretch to call this a conversion; the only remaining original features are the roof trusses, now painted a vivid green to distinguish them from the new light-coloured glulam beams that give the house its structural integrity.

However, Hall & Bednarczyk's building is resoundingly barn-like, thanks to its simple linear shape, black corrugated metal roof and timber cladding. The outside is cedar, weathered to a silvery colour that helps the building melt into its surroundings; in the large entrance porch, with its generous wood store to feed the stove inside, the walls are the original rich russet shade, unblemished by the weather.

Inside the single-storey structure, the full-height open eaves and largely open-plan layout – with a large kitchen-dining-lounging area at one end and the bedrooms at the other – make for light, airy living spaces. Hanging sliding barn doors maintain the uncluttered look and hark back to the building's agricultural roots. A limited palette of colours and materials has been used, with white painted walls (either plastered or, for a bit more textural interest, covered with tongue-and-groove panelling) and near-black polished concrete floors – with underfloor heating for comfort underfoot. The timber elements, from the dining table to the coat hooks, unite outside and in, and add essential warmth to what might otherwise feel a bit clinical.

An admirer of Scandinavian design for its simplicity and modernity, Sue has furnished The Chickenshed with contemporary furniture in black, green and timber from Danish companies. The zingy moss/lime green sofa was the reason why the beams were painted green: Sue had already ordered the furniture and couldn't find a suitable colour, so thought it would be better if they matched. As it happens, it looks like it was meant to be, with the grass green picking up on the landscape outside. The furniture either has a visual lightness about it – such as the dining chairs, with their

beech-ply seats folding into the legs like butterfly wings – or is monolithic and free from excess adornment, like the chunky sofas.

The kitchen is snowy white, disappearing into its surroundings, and there are no wall cabinets, making the space feel as un-kitchen-like as possible. Simple wooden shelving cuts across the kitchen windows, providing open storage that is beautifully silhouetted against the daylight.

As well as the Scandinavian influence, there is local craftsmanship here, too. Sue commissioned Hay-on-Wye-based furniture-maker Rob Barnby to make the trestle-style oak dining table and upholstered bench seating, both constructed to exactly fit the available space. Rob also made the simple platform beds with storage underneath – Sue had looked for a neat storage bed that would fit her pared-back aesthetic but couldn't find anything, so Rob came to the rescue with a design that seems to float above the floor yet is also incredibly practical. The timber bedside storage boxes and bedside lighting are wall mounted, helping to keep the space feeling clutter-free and to retain a sense of orderliness. It's not all minimalism, though. Cosy Welsh Carthenni blankets on the beds let guests know exactly where they are – tucked in the bosom of nature, deep in the Wye Valley.

PURELY FUNCTIONAL

Kitchens can sometimes look fussy in otherwise plain, open-plan spaces. The solution here is to make the units unobtrusive, with handle-free cupboards and a uniform white finish (right). What catches the eye instead are the warm timber elements, such as the objects on the wooden shelves across the window.

COUNTRY CONTEMPORARY

Tongue-and-groove panelling alludes to the building's agricultural roots and also provides some textural interest on an otherwise unadorned wall. The steel beams are the only element that survives from the old chicken shed and have been painted green to highlight them (above right). The dining table and bench seating below was made by local craftsman Rob Barnby, while the chairs with their wing-like seats in moulded plywood are from a contemporary Danish design company (opposite). Wooden bowls on the kitchen shelves are bathed in light from the window (above left).

WARM INTRODUCTION

The generous entrance area sets up the feeling of spaciousness that is characteristic of the whole house (opposite). Hanging sliding doors aren't just an eminently appropriate style for a converted chicken shed – they're also a neater way to divide up large open spaces than a hinged version (above). Colourful Welsh blankets pick up on the green that is echoed around the rest of the interior, as well as providing a sense of place (above right); the platform beds with built-in storage were made by local craftsman Rob Barnby. Vintage bags hang from the Danish coat hooks, their time-worn appearance emphasized by the pristine white wall (right).

WIND HOUSE

Architect Flemming Skude compares his home to a Viking ship; like a boat on the water, its curving shape works with the elements rather than against them. The house, on the Danish island of Lolland in the Baltic Sea, is exposed to southwesterly gusts, so instead of choosing a box shape that would cause turbulent wind flow, the 'prow' of the building faces straight into the weather. This also gives the house its name – Wind House.

Like a Viking ship, Wind House is made from wood, inside and out. It replaced an older house on the site, and is used by Flemming and his family as a retreat from city life in Copenhagen, a couple of hours away. Lolland has wide skies and open spaces, and the wind makes the trees grow flat and low in a wedge shape – another inspiration for the form of Flemming's house.

As a piece of craftsmanship, the house is outstanding, but its beautiful finish was hard-won. It took four years for Flemming to develop the plans for the house and six months to build it, with two skilled carpenters on site creating the curving cedar exterior and larch roof. Pine is the traditional material used here for rural cabins, but it requires painting or sealing, whereas Flemming's choice reflects a more sustainable approach, since larch and cedar are longer-lasting and will not require chemical treatment.

Pitch-pine cladding on the interior walls gives the house the cosy, enveloping feel of a traditional Scandinavian cabin, while its curved walls and dramatically pitched ceilings make it more interesting and unexpected. It sticks to a limited palette of materials – timber walls, whitewashed ceilings and linoleum floors – which is both soothing on the eye and gives the house the feel of a giant piece of sculpture. Flemming's eye for the sculptural extends to the fact that he is a sculptor himself – his carved wooden pieces can be found dotted around the house, offering an idiosyncratic contrast to the geometry of the curves and straight lines of the architecture.

Flemming says that his affinity with wood springs from the fact that "it feels warm and smooth when touched – in contrast to steel and concrete – and it also has a more *hyggelig* [cosy] inviting look. Wood is also a friendly material to work with, and smells wonderful."

There are playful elements to the house – it is a weekend retreat after all, built for leisure and family time. A zigzagging open staircase leads up to a cabin-like retreat for Flemming's grandson – the architect says he designed it without a handrail to teach his grandchildren "that life is dangerous". In the room at the top of the stairs, there is a peekaboo hatch that overlooks the curved corridor off which the bedrooms sit, and the leaf-shaped corridor below is a smaller-scale version of the footprint of the house itself.

The furnishings are beautifully simple: woven rugs and beds that are just a platform on the floor. Storage is built into the thickness of the walls to

A simple palette of materials could look austere, but Flemming has included plenty of intriguing details to keep things lively. Getting from A to B is more interesting when it means travelling along curvy corridors or mounting zigzagging open steps (opposite). The little hiding place at the top of the stairs, with its square opening, was built for Flemming's grandson so he can act as a lookout (left).

minimize clutter – the focus is either on the architecture itself, or the views outside. Despite the lack of 'stuff', the house doesn't seem hard or cold, mostly because of the warmth that the timber-clad walls bring, and because it feels so obviously crafted by human hands. There are softer textures too, such as sheepskin-clad chairs and a sofa piled with cushions, set around a wood-burning stove. Most of the furniture is old, brought from the former house on the site or Flemming's home in Copenhagen, which makes the place feel lived-in.

Some of the rooms lead straight outside into the house's verdant surroundings; the garden is loose and untamed, blending into the woodland beyond. Despite its very modern appearance and striking curved shape, the house sits very well in its setting, not least because of the use of natural materials. Flemming has managed to cleverly minimize less attractive practical elements such as guttering, so that all there is to see is the house's simple curved form. Wind House is as sculptural on the outside as it is within.

DRAMATIC HEIGHTS

The building's sharply sloping ceilings bring a sense of drama, as well as a feeling of spaciousness, to the open-plan kitchen (opposite). Much of the furniture, such as the classic stick-back dining chairs, Flemming owned already, making the space look instantly lived-in despite the newness of the architecture. The eye-level kitchen cupboards are made from pitch pine to blend in with the wall cladding (above left). Bedrooms are sparsely furnished, with simple platform beds and concealed storage, drawing the eye directly out to the garden (above right).

SWEEPING CURVES
Faded to a multi-tonal grey, the cedar house
has a feeling of serenity about it, thanks to its
sculptural curves and unfussy exterior. Flemming
has concealed some features, such as the guttering.

WHITECROSS FARM

We live and work at Whitecross Farm just outside Ross-on-Wye in the Herefordshire countryside. The 18th-century farmhouse is our home and overlooks the barns that house our homeware store. The woody things that we sell at the farm are reflected in the objects that we surround ourselves with at home, and they all share our philosophy of being plain, simple and useful.

Unlike many of the homes featured in this book, our house is not made from wood – it is sandstone, with lath and plaster internal walls – but nonetheless we have filled it with wooden furniture and objects of every size and origin. In the hallway, for example, which has undergone countless makeovers, there are blackened ware boards and old shop signs lining the walls, while lamps made from bobbins and plumbers' beads hang down over the shelf. On the shelf, side by side, stand wooden exercise pins, pork pie moulds, turned bowls and hat blocks. We are attracted to anything with a sculptural shape, a curious history or the patina of age (sometimes all three) and love the unexpected juxtaposition of putting a found wooden object next to a decorative one, or a weather-bleached piece of oak alongside a russet-toned hardwood.

The loft has become a laboratory of ideas and experiment. With its exposed timber rafters, it is packed with woody collections destined for the store: Swedish chairs hang from the trusses and groups of old wooden print blocks line the floor. There are further collections of timber items in the studio: more hat blocks, coin trays, French butter spoons and wooden sculptural objects. In one corner is an old Chesterfield sofa, stripped back to reveal its skeletal wooden framework, and an old tripod converted into a lamp.

Timber features more prominently in the kitchen, which has recently undergone an undecorated makeover. The kitchen island is an old French shop counter, complete with original till drawer, which we bought in Barjac in southern France. A workbench has been converted into a sink stand, above which hangs a fairground ball game. The massive pitch-pine estate dresser/ hutch that runs along one wall is filled with French studio pottery and sycamore plates by Ray Key, with wooden French grape boxes underneath to house cookware and baking dishes.

The house is always in a state of flux, but our latest acquisition is a little more permanent. Sandwiched between the farmhouse and the workshop is Molly, a 1950s showman's van we spotted advertised in the window of a newsagent in Hay-on-Wye. Despite being built for a nomadic lifestyle, Molly is local – we found her marooned in a farmyard just outside Staunton on Arrow, looking slightly the worse for wear.

Restoring her was a painstaking task and took almost three years. She is built entirely of wood except for an external aluminium skin and steel trailer. Our first task was to repair the roof and make her watertight by stripping off layers of asphalt and replacing them with lead. We then took out all the internal panelling, repairing the framework and insulating the walls with sheep's wool. (The coins and wishbones found in the original framework, traditionally put in for luck, were all carefully returned.) Unsafe gas lighting was replaced with electric. We machined new tongue-and-groove boarding in our workshop and panelled the interior, then renewed the floor using old floorboards.

Our final task was to install an Esse Ironheart wood-burning stove for heating and cooking. A simple kitchen uses an old shop counter for the work surface and bench seating that doubles as an extra sleeping area with storage underneath. Though we have yet to spend the night in her, we have had a Christening party with our grandchildren. Molly is ready for her next journey.

WELSH DRESSER

This enormous pitch-pine dresser/hutch sits at the heart of the kitchen (right); it came from a large Welsh country estate, and we use it to display our collection of studio pottery from the 1960s and '70s, as well as sycamore plates by woodturner Ray Key. The French grape-harvest bins slotted in underneath the drawers store cookware and baking dishes.

INDUSTRIAL HERITAGE

One of our sheds has been repurposed as a space to think and work. It's also the overspill for the tea room at the store – hence it also seemed an appropriate place to display some of our collection of Brown Betty teapots from the Stoke potteries (above). The machinists' chairs, sourced from textile mills in Yorkshire, are evocative of Britain's industrial past, and are comfortable, too (opposite). A light made by Mark was created from old belt-driven cogs, topped with a bulb (above right). These brightly coloured metal stools were once tractor seats – their unusual shape give them a striking silhouette (right).

SIMPLE SHAPES

A French 19th-century sofa has been stripped back to reveal its frame – an indigo kapok mattress and some cushions are all it needed to restore its comfort (above left). We made this simple fireplace surround from scrap wood that was originally used as architrave and skirting/base board, and still boasts its original white paint (above right). In the bay window stands part of our large collection of furniture from Ethiopia, including bowl-shaped three-legged stools and high-backed chairs – the maker's hand is very apparent in their idiosyncratic shapes and roughly carved surface (opposite). The graphic textile hanging behind the chairs is a Kuba cloth from the former Zaire; these handwoven and naturally dyed fabrics are prized for their complex detail.

FREEDOM TO EXPERIMENT

The hallway is always in a state of flux, its run of low shelving providing the ideal platform for experimentation. Here it's shown with a marching regiment of exercise pins, pork pie moulds, hat blocks and bowls, set against a wall of vertically stacked ware boards and shop signage (opposite). A single plank of teak discovered in a boat yard in Cornwall forms a headboard, its deeply textured grain looking like ripples across water (above left). Open rails display clothing in our dressing room, against a backdrop of sawn timber-clad walls (above right).

A TEMPLE TO TIMBER

The loft is packed to its woody rafters with timber objects, including Swedish chairs hanging from the beams and Ethiopian saddle stools sitting under the workbench. A ship's rope ladder tumbles out of a basket in the foreground (opposite). Elsewhere, old wooden floats look invitingly sculptural on the windowsill (above right), while hat blocks are lined up on a shelf (above far right). This is part of our collection of printing blocks (far right). A curated display of wooden objects is united by their common material – an aeroplane chock, carved Ethiopian and Rajasthani panels, a paddle and a wooden bicycle wheel (right).

TRAVELLING VAN

Molly is our 1950s showman's van, meticulously restored over three years (above). Under her aluminium external skin, she is entirely made from wood, with replacement tongue-and-groove panelling and reclaimed floorboards. A folding wooden table is one of the many space-saving ideas used in Molly's interior and there is also hidden storage under the seats (opposite above left). The Ironheart range opposite the kitchen prep area keeps the van warm (opposite above and below right). The beds wear airy white Baileys linen, while a tea chest serves as a bedside table/night stand (opposite below left).

THE BOAT HOUSE

Nestled into the volcanic coastal landscape of Stokkseyri in southern Iceland, Kristinn Arnarson and Rut Káradóttir's seaside getaway is a paradise for birdwatchers and lovers of nature. Barn House is a modern take on a traditional agricultural building, built in 2010 for a retired ship engineer who commissioned his son, an architect, to build him a home that would offer more than a hint of his maritime past. Kristinn and Rut bought the place in 2015, after they saw it advertised for sale in a newspaper. They already knew the house and its surroundings well, as they frequently visited the area to eat at a favourite restaurant, which is 45 minutes from their main home in Reykjavik.

Rut is an interior designer, and at Barn House she has combined Nordic design with Japanese influences to create a serene, modern interior. There are some subtle nautical touches, too, such as the porthole mirror and porcelain cabin lights. The couple have imagined the house as a ship: the two floors are the 'upper deck' and 'lower deck', and the balcony facing into the North Atlantic is 'the bridge'. The staircase connecting the two floors is also quite ship-like, and can be closed off completely to create a tranquil retreat.

Like a beautifully crafted yacht, the interior is made from wood. All the walls are clad in birch-faced plywood, a material that brings both crisp, angular modernity and a light, warm feel. The flooring is brushed Siberian larch, but the hall, bathroom and another ground-floor room have been coated with a layer of rich, nutty brown shell sand from the beach in front of the house, blurring the boundaries between inside and out.

Collections of tactile objects bring the house to life: baskets and bowls sit on the open shelves in the kitchen, with Danish hand-made ceramic plates and mugs. Soft furnishings such as cushions, blankets and a reindeer skin bring a further layer of tactility. The colours are subtle and natural, echoing the landscape outside. Rut has sourced far and wide, from contemporary European makers to flea-market finds and throws brought back from Morocco. Some objects she had owned for a while, such as the wooden pestle and mortar, which was bought in Finland. The art has a family connection: a landscape painting above the shower-room sink was created by Rut's nephew when he was ten years old, and her father painted the work that hangs in the master bedroom.

The building's volcanic surroundings provide design inspiration, too. A lava stone is used as an object to be displayed and admired, and the kitchen, made by a local carpenter, has a matt finish in 'lava grey' speckled with green – a visual echo of the 100-year-old moss-covered stone and turf wall that runs along the front of the house. As with the majority of Icelandic homes, geothermal energy heats the house and electricity is generated by a hydroelectric power station.

Volcanic stone also features in the architecture. A plinth of rough-hewn blocks forms the lower level of the house with the Siberian larch cladding rising up from it, providing a smooth, ordered contrast to the stone wall. The architecture may have some traditional features, such as the ground-floor barn doors and shuttered window above it, but it is resolutely different to the traditional local houses with their rendered walls and bright red roofs.

There is a slow pace of life here in Stokkseyri. Seals, birds and sometimes the fin of a whale can be spotted directly from the house (a view that can be magnified with the aid of a telescope), and there are plenty of corners for reading and places for lounging. Best of all, the revered lobster restaurant Fjöruborðið – the reason why the couple were regular visitors to the area in the first place – is no longer a 45-minute drive away but just a short stroll.

SHIP SHAPE

The staircase is boat-like in its design, with a raised hatch (above left); lacquered kitchen cabinets are painted in a green-grey speckled finish to harmonize with the moss-covered walls outside (above right); the whole house is lined with knot-free plywood, creating a cosy, tranquil backdrop (opposite).

BRINGING THE OUTSIDE IN

A colour scheme of greens, greys and blues has been chosen to echo the palette of the natural world beyond the glass (opposite). Slim, minimal shower fittings echo the vertical lines of the timber-lined enclosure (above left); modern metal hooks create a strong graphic outline against the plywood (left); the bathroom floor is made from hardened shell sand, gathered from the adjacent beach (above).

OUT IN THE COLD
Built from Siberian larch, the house
is designed to withstand Iceland's
testing climate (this page and
opposite). Traditional architectural
elements, such as the barn doors
and shutters, give little clue as to
the modern interior.

INTO
THE WOODS

It may resemble an ancient hunting lodge, but Antonio Bembo and Anda Hobai's house is actually a delightful illusion. The pillars on the porch are 200 years old, but the house itself was built only a few years ago, a clever fusion of new construction and reclaimed materials.

The couple live in Breaza, Romania (Antonio is Italian; Anda is Romanian), a tiny village an hour and a half's drive north-west of Bucharest. Antonio owns a business specializing in embroidered clothing for luxury brands, and Anda is an architect and life coach. They were already settled here when neighbours put up for sale a plot of land adjacent to their home. The couple snapped it up and built a new house next to their current one, which is where they still live day to day. The lodge is the place they go to switch off, and where they have indulged their love of traditional craftsmanship.

Antonio is a hunter who dreamed of walls hung with trophies, while Anda has always been fascinated by Romanian architecture and crafts, and as a student used to spend hours at Bucharest's National Village Museum, an ethnographic museum of traditional rural life. Long before the neighbouring land came up for sale, the couple had started collecting items for their own vision of a traditional home – including those 200-year-old pillars – and Antonio would salvage objects such as shutters and window frames from abandoned buildings he came across on his hunting trips.

Local craftsmen built the house using traditional construction methods. It took more than two years, which gave the couple time to source everything required to make it seem like the place had centuries of history behind it, such as the flooring for the main living space, which came from an Italian reclamation specialist, and the traditional Romanian ceramic stove that dominates one corner of the room – it's new, but made to a design that hasn't changed in 500 years.

Friends dug around in their cellars and lofts to find pieces that might work in the new property, and the couple engaged the help of another friend, architect Silvio Stefani, to help them track down antiques and reclaimed materials. Silvio also introduced some contemporary design ideas, such as the heated concrete platform in the 'silence room', where the couple go to relax after using the sauna, and the enormous curling metal chandeliers that fill the main living space.

This space is dominated by a whole tree trunk, soaring up through the centre of the room. Some of the visible timber framing on the walls is structural; some of it purely decorative. There are examples of Romanian crafts here, such as the rugs and the painted furniture from Transylvania, but Antonio and Anda have cast their net wider than that, mounting an antique painted ceiling panel from Venice on the wall and including leather armchairs from a French antiques shop.

Signs of modern life have been cleverly concealed: the refrigerator and dishwasher are encased in old timber, while outside the logs stacked against a vast wall are not, in fact, used for the stove, but are purely a dramatic way to cover up the side of the garage. The extraordinary bathtub and basin in the bathroom were made from hollowed-out tree trunks that were originally antique dough or feeding troughs. They were sent away to have a resin layer applied on the inside to make them smooth and watertight then holes were drilled, wastes fitted and metal feet were added to the bathtub to make it fully functional.

Anda and Antonio have gone to such great lengths to get every detail correct that in centuries to come the lodge itself may end up at Bucharest's National Village Museum.

A ROVING EYE

Although many of the items furnishing the house were sourced from Romania, Anda and Antonio also looked further afield. The patchwork of faded painted panels on one wall was once part of a ceiling in a Venetian home (above), and both the cinema chairs, and the old leather armchairs were found in a French antiques shop (opposite and overleaf).

DISTRESSED SURFACES

Architect Silvio Stefani suggested that Anda and Antonio should add some modern materials and industrial elements to their interiors to prevent the house looking like a pastiche. The bare-bulb lighting (above left) and distressed-concrete splashback above the sink (above right) are two examples of this, offering a contrast to the warm, brown tones of the reclaimed kitchen units and copper pans. The glazed doors leading to the kitchen may look old, but they are in fact brand new – the metal frames were treated to give them an aged, rusted look and then sealed so that they won't degrade any further (opposite).

QUIET SPACE

The 'silence room' is where the couple restore themselves after visiting the sauna; this spare, minimal space is perfect for relaxation and contemplation, and features a concrete plinth with a mattress-shaped well in the middle for a water-bed (opposite). The crisp, square lines of the concrete are in contrast to the knotty grained shutters and gnarled beams. A staircase is made from 200-year-old Romanian wood (above left). It leads up to an attic bedroom that is used as a guest room – decorative detail is kept to a minimum here so that the characterful old beams become the focal point (above right).

AWASH WITH DETAIL
The extraordinary bathtub is an old Romanian dough trough – these were once common, but more recently have been left outdoors and used as feeding troughs (opposite). Anda and Antonio had the tub lined with a tough resin coating to make it waterproof and set it on metal legs. Elsewhere in the bathroom, open rails turn clothing into objects of display (above far left). A shallow stone sink has a pitted surface that picks up on the texture of the concrete splashback (above left), while a narrow wooden bench strikes an imperfect note in the clean-lined shower room (left). Metal hooks and handles are silhouetted against the wooden wall cladding (far left).

OUTWARD EXPRESSION

The enormous log store takes up a whole wall of the outside of the building and makes an incredible feature (left). The hefty square pillars running along the exterior are 200-year-old timbers and the V-shaped metal brace at the top of each one is a traditional Romanian architectural detail (below). Many of the doors and shutters were bought from salvage yards in Romania (opposite).

THE PLOUGH

This is a house that has already had several previous incarnations. Originally a smallholding, it spent much of the last century as a pub called The Plough before reverting to a private home. Owners Matt and Clare have taken a considered, thoughtful approach to its restoration; it has taken seven years so far and is still a work in progress.

The house is located in Herefordshire's Golden Valley. This is cider country, and the local agricultural history forms part of the fabric of the building – apples were grown on the surrounding land and the outbuildings were used to press the cider. The old apple store is now the couple's living room with a guest bedroom above. There is also a reminder of the house's past as a pub – the built-in settle in the kitchen. The kitchen walls resemble a Turneresque stormy seascape, the result of stripping them back to reveal layers of bright blue paint (a colour traditionally used in kitchens to ward off insects).

Matt has done much of the building and renovation work himself, drawing on his training as a conservation stonemason to create something sympathetic to the house's history and character. Clare is a Pilates instructor, but they both trained as sculptors and have lately found themselves returning to artistic pursuits; the sculptors' approach to respecting materials while drawing out the best in them is very evident here. Objects are chosen for their sculptural qualities, their raw material or their patina. One example of this are the stacked-up cardboard boxes that were once used to store electrical components to fix telephone junction boxes; they were inherited from Clare's great aunt, who worked for the GPO in the Second World War and subsequently used them for storing her embroidery threads.

There is an honesty to the way things are presented in the house – services are on show, not hidden away. Electrical cables are attached to the wall rather than chased into it; the copper header tank for the gravity-fed water system is mounted on the wall in the bedroom with copper pipes snaking down the wall – Clare says it reminds her of a mad scientist's lab from a black and white film.

Reclamation and reuse of materials can be seen everywhere. Salvaged oak timbers from Clare and Matt's previous property have been used as lintels, for example, and floorboards from one room now form the cladding for a partition wall at the top of the stairs. The sliding barn doors were also made from scrap oak floorboards, and the guest bedroom that was once the apple store features a headboard constructed from a wattle and daub panel. Reclaimed materials not only add to the textures and layers of history of the interiors, but this approach has been chosen for financial expediency as well: even the smallest scraps of leftover wood go to feed the wood-burning stove.

New timbers added to the building during the restoration have been painted with a limewash made with fire ash and natural pigments, helping

them to blend with the original wood. There is a chalky softness to the walls that is both tactile and calming, with a pleasing contrast between the rough, bumpy ancient walls and the silky new tadelakt plaster.

All the senses are engaged in Clare and Matt's house. Scent is important to them, and they frequently burn sticks of Palo Santo – a mystical South American tree related to frankincense and myrrh, and associated with healing and cleansing – or incense from Prinknash Abbey, made by the monks there for more than a century.

There is a sense of calm and quietness to Clare and Matt's house, which is perhaps surprising given that it was once such a bustling social hub. As Clare says, "Considering it has a history of many visitors coming and going, having operated as a pub for so many years, it feels like it is breathing out now. The calm after the storm."

SOLID STATE

Trained sculptors Clare and Matt say their love of material and form has informed the aesthetic of their home. In the kitchen, rustic furniture enhances the ancient character of the former pub (above left and right). Exposed stone walls and flagstone floors give a feeling of solidity and permanence. Matt made the sliding door from scrap oak floorboards (opposite).

GENTLE TEXTURES
The view through a crooked door frame into the kitchen, where the original sky blue wall paint was uncovered during Clare and Matt's ongoing restoration of the house (opposite). The simple stove has a cast-concrete hearth stone (this page). Limewashing has given the walls a cloudy appearance with layers of depth and texture.

SENSORY REFLECTION

Pipes and electrical conduits are largely left on show rather than hidden away, including this copper water tank with its snaking pipework in one of the bedrooms (above left and right). Burning aromatic sticks of Basilica incense helps to satisfy all the senses (right). In this airy bedroom, which was once an apple store, a wattle and daub oak panel has been turned into a headboard (opposite).

PICTURE CREDITS

All photographs by Debi Treloar, except where stated.

Endpapers and 1 The Oslo home of designer/maker Heidi Bjørnsdotter of volt.no; 2–3 Clare and Matt in Herefordshire; 4–5 The home of Mark and Sally Bailey of baileyshome.com; 6 The Oslo home of designer/maker Heidi Bjørnsdotter of volt.no; 7 photograph by Mark Bailey; 8 left A cabin in Norway designed and owned by Marianne and Jon Vigtel Hølland of slowdesign.no; 8 right–9 The home of Mark and Sally Bailey of baileyshome.com; 11 The Oslo home of designer/maker Heidi Bjørnsdotter of volt.no; 12–13 The home of Mark and Sally Bailey of baileyshome.com; 14 The home in Oslo of designer/maker Heidi Bjørnsdotter of volt.no; 15 left and centre The Oslo home of designer/maker Heidi Bjørnsdotter of volt.no; 15 right Interior designers Stefan and Jeanette Walther of home-interior.de; 16 above left Interior designers Stefan and Jeanette Walther of home-interior.de; 16 above right and below The home of Mark and Sally Bailey of baileyshome.com; 17 A cabin in Norway designed and owned by Marianne and Jon Vigtel Hølland of slowdesign.no; 18 The home of Mark and Sally Bailey of baileyshome.com; 19 Alex and Danielle Hoda; Hollyhocks Cottage can be rented through uniquehomestays.com; 20 left The home of Antonio Bembo and Anda Hobai in Romania; 20 centre The home of Mark and Sally Bailey of baileyshome.com; 20 right and 21 The Chickenshed is available to rent at thechickeshedatparkhouse.com; 22 Architect Flemming Skude, Denmark; 23 above left The Chickenshed is available to rent at thechickenshedatparkhouse.com; 23 above right A cabin in Norway designed and owned by Marianne and Jon Vigtel Hølland slowdesign.no; 23 below The home of Mark and Sally Bailey of baileyshome.com; 24 left Clare and Matt in Herefordshire; 24 right and 25 The Barn House in Iceland husrum.is; 26 Alex and Danielle Hoda; Hollyhocks Cottage can be rented through uniquehomestays.com; 27 A cabin in Norway designed and owned by Marianne and Jon Vigtel Hølland of slowdesign.no; 28 The home of Antonio Bembo and Anda Hobai in Romania; 29 left The home of Mark and Sally Bailey of baileyshome.com; 29 right A cabin in Norway designed and owned by Marianne and Jon Vigtel Hølland of slowdesign.no; 30 Interior designers Stefan and Jeanette Walther of home-interior.de; 31 The home of Mark and Sally Bailey of baileyshome.com; 32 Artist/designer Jo Guinness; 33 left and right Artist/designer Jo Guinness; 33 centre Clare and Matt in Herefordshire; 34 Clare and Matt in Herefordshire; 35 Artist/designer Jo Guinness; 36–37 The home of Antonio Bembo and Anda Hobai in Romania; 38–39 The home of Mark and Sally Bailey of baileyshome.com; 40 left and below right The home of Mark and Sally Bailey of baileyshome.com; 40 above right The home of Mark and Sally Bailey of baileyshome.com; 41 The home of Mark and Sally Bailey of baileyshome.com; 42–43 Artist/designer Jo Guinness; 44–57 A cabin in Norway designed and owned by Marianne and Jon Vigtel Hølland of slowdesign.no; 58–68 The home of Mark and Sally Bailey of baileyshome.com; 69 Debi Treloar for Baileys; 70–79 Interior designers Stefan and Jeanette Walther of home-interior.de; 80–89 Artist/designer Jo Guinness; 90–99 Alex and Danielle Hoda; Hollyhocks Cottage can be rented through uniquehomestays.com; 100–109 The Oslo home of designer/maker Heidi Bjørnsdotter of volt.no; 110–117 The Chickenshed is available to rent at thechickeshedatparkhouse.com; 118–125 Architect Flemming Skude, Denmark; 126–139 The home of Mark and Sally Bailey of baileyshome.com; 140–147 The Barn House in Iceland www.husrum.is; 148–161 The home of Antonio Bembo and Anda Hobai in Romania; 162–169 Clare and Matt in Herefordshire; 168 below photograph: Mark Bailey; 172 The home of Mark and Sally Bailey of baileyshome.com; 175 Interior designers Stefan and Jeanette Walther of home-interior.de; 176 The Oslo home of designer/maker Heidi Bjørnsdotter of volt.no.

BUSINESS CREDITS

Mark and Sally Bailey
Baileys Home
Whitecross Farm
Bridstow
Ross-on-Wye
Herefordshire HR9 6JU
baileyshome.com
Pages 4, 5, 8 right, 9, 12, 13, 16 above right, 16 below, 18, 20 centre, 23 below, 29 left, 31, 38, 39, 40 left, 40 below right, 40 above right, 41, 58–68, 69, 126–139, 172.

The Barn House
Architect:
Hallgrimur Björnsson
Interior Designer:
Rut Káradóttir
rutkara.is
The Barn House is available to rent at husrum.is
Pages 24 right, 25, 140–147.

Heidi Bjørnsdotter
volt.no
Endpapers, 1, 6, 11, 14, 15 left, 15 centre, 100–109, 176.

The Chickenshed
The Chickenshed is available to rent at
E: info@
thechickenshedatparkhouse.
   com
thechickenshedatparkhouse.
   com
Architects:
Hall & Bednarczyk
12a Lower Church Street

Chepstow NP16 5HJ
T: +44 (0)1291 627777
hallbednarczyk.com
Pages 20 right, 21, 23 above left, 110–117.

Jo Guinness
T: 07803 016 916
E: joguinness@icloud.com
Pages 32, 33 left, 33 right, 35, 42–43 80–89.

Alex and Danielle Hoda
Hollyhocks Cottage is available to rent at
uniquehomestays.com
Pages 19, 26, 90–99.

Marianne Vigtel Hølland
Slow Design Studio
Instagram: @slow_design
slowdesign.no
Architect:
Benedicte Sund-Mathisen
Suma Arkitektur
Pages 8 left, 17, 23 above right, 27, 29 right, 44–57.

Flemming Skude
flemmingskude.com
Pages 22, 118–125.

Stefan and Jeanette Walther
J.W. Home-Interior GmbH
Mittelstrasse 45
45549 Sprockhövel-
   Haßlinghausen
Germany
T: +49 (0)2339 124300
E: info@home-interior.de
home-interior.de
Pages 15 right, 16 above left, 30, 70–79, 175.

ADDRESS BOOK

UK SOURCES

Baileys Home Store
Whitecross Farm
Bridstow
Ross-on-Wye
Herefordshire HR9 6JU
+44 (0)1989 561931
Baileyshome.com
*Our store, always full of
wooden wonders.*

Bauwerk Colour
Bauwerkcolour.co.uk
*Modern lime paint that does
not harm the environment.*

Caro Somerset
18–20 High Street
Bruton
Somerset BA10 0AA
carosomerset.com
*Carefully chosen objects
sourced from around the globe.*

Cart-House
Cart-house.com
*Ben and Cathryn Bailey,
our son and daughter-in-law,
specialize in early- to mid-
20th-century furniture.*

The Crafts Council
craftscouncil.org.uk
*National agency for the
development of contemporary
craft in the UK. Visit their
website for a directory of craft
and makers in the UK.*

Devol
Devolkitchens.co.uk
Hand-made wooden kitchens.

Hole & Corner
Holeandcorner.com
*Quarterly magazine
celebrating creativity,
craftsmanship and heritage.*

Joined + Jointed
1 New Kings Road
London SW6 4SB
+44 (0)20 7371 7766
joinedandjointed.com
*A collective of contemporary
furniture designers.*

Midgley Green
26 Alexandra Road
Clevedon
North Somerset BS21 7QH
+44 (0)1275 871989
Midgleygreen.com
*Beautifully crafted homewares
hand-made in Britain.*

The New Craftsmen
34 North Row
London W1K 6DG
+44 (0)20 7148 3190
thenewcraftsmen.com
*Carefully curated selection
of British craft.*

Osmo
osmouk.com
*Natural oil and wax-based
finishes.*

Pinch Design
46 Bourne Street
London SW1W 8JD
+44 (0)20 7622 5075
Pinchdesign.com
*Russell Pinch and Oonagh
Bannon design and make
furniture and lighting.*

Plain English
Plainenglish.co.uk
Bespoke hand-made kitchens.

SCP
scp.co.uk
*Modern, lasting, timeless
furniture.*

Ty-Mawr Lime
+44 (0)1874 611350
lime.org.uk
*Lime paint and traditional
building materials.*

Woodworks by Ted Todd
79 Margaret Street
London W1W 8TA
+44 (0)20 7495 6706
Woodworksbytedtodd.com
*Antique and reclaimed
wooden flooring.*

UK MAKERS

Barnby Design
barnbydesign.co.uk
*Simply designed furniture made
in a barn near Hay-on-Wye.*

Benchmark
Bath Road
Kinbury
Hungerford
Berkshire RG17 9SA
benchmarkfurniture.com
*Designers and makers of
contemporary furniture.*

Alice Blogg
aliceblogg.co.uk
*Designer and maker creating
functional and tactile pieces.*

Byron and Gómez
byronandgomez.co.uk
*Designer-makers creating
hand-crafted furniture in
their workshop in Somerset.*

Paul Caton
paulcaton.com
*Wood carver and sculptor
creating pieces for domestic
settings as well as hotels
and restaurants.*

Sebastian Cox
sebastiancox.co.uk
*Contemporary furniture made
from fallen trees, offcuts and
coppiced timber.*

Established & Sons
establishedandsons.com
*Iconic and innovative British
design company.*

Forest + Found
forestandfound.com
*Woodworkers Max Bainbridge
and Abigail Booth produce
beautiful wooden vessels
and sculptures.*

Hope in the Woods
hopeinthewoods.com
*Elegant, minimalist wooden
vessels, platters and bowls
hand-carved by Luke Hope.*

Knowles and Christou
knowles-christou.com
*Nature-inspired hand-printed
fabrics and wallpaper.*

John Makepeace
johnmakepeacefurniture.com
*Renowned designer and
furniture maker.*

Tom Raffield
tomraffield.com
*Contemporary steam-bent
lighting and furniture designed
and made in Cornwall.*

James Tattersall
jtattersall.co.uk
*Hand-made furniture with
clean, contemporary feel.*

Temper Studio
temperstudio.com
*Contemporary furniture and
kitchenware made to order in
a small workshop in Wiltshire.*

Jan Waterston
janwaterston.co.uk
Contemporary furniture.

Will Elworthy.
willelworthy.co.uk
*Woodturner and furniture
maker creating turned items
and bespoke pieces.*

The Windsor Workshop
thewindsorworkshop.co.uk
*James Mursell makes chairs
and runs chairmaking
workshops in West Sussex.*

Robin Wood
robin-wood.co.uk
*Makes wooden bowls
on a foot-powered lathe.*

Wooden & Woven
Woodwoven.com
*Hand-crafted pieces
by Alexander Devol.*

USA

Allen Booth
allenbooth.com
*Well-made goods for your
kitchen and your home.*

Brooklyn Makers
brooklynmakers.com
*A blog championing local
talent, hand-made quality
and responsible manufacturing.*

Etsy
etsy.com
*A worldwide marketplace
for craftspeople and makers.*

Factory 20
factory20.com
Vintage industrial furniture.

HomeStories
homestories.com
*Beautifully simple baskets,
wooden kitchenware and
linen bedding.*

Salvage One
1840 W Hubbard Street
Chicago, IL 60622
312 733 0098
salvageone.com
*Recycled furniture, accessories
and collectibles, including old
wooden doors and antique
wooden furniture.*

JAPANESE

Analogue Life
analoguelife.com
*Beautifully crafted products
hand-made by artisans.*

Fog Linen
foglinen.com
*Mango-wood bowls and
utensils, occasional makers'
pop-ups and workshops.*

Found Muji
muji.com/sg/foundmuji/
*Simple, useful, everyday items
from different cultures.*

Outbound
outbound.to
*Lifestyle store hosting
changing exhibitions and
selling carved furniture, woven
baskets and fine textiles.*

Ryuji Mitani
mitaniryuji.com
*Japan's most celebrated
woodworker.*

Yoshiaki Tadaki
www.yoshiakitadaki.com
*This wood artist hand-carves
wooden cutlery, bowls and
utensils at his workshop.*

INDEX

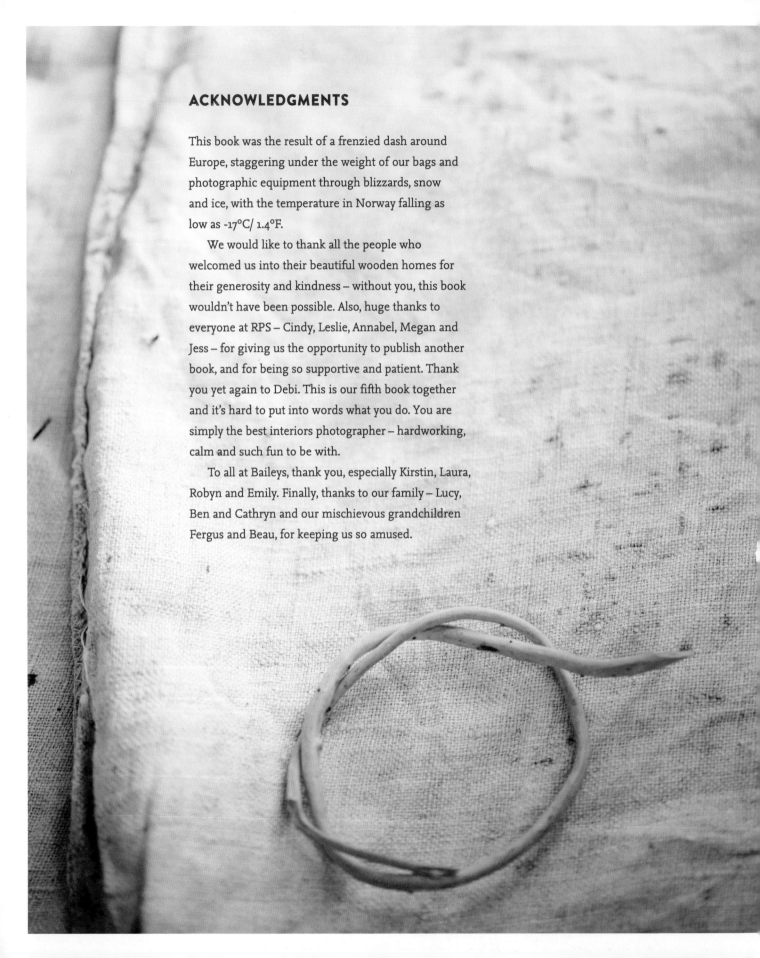

ACKNOWLEDGMENTS

This book was the result of a frenzied dash around Europe, staggering under the weight of our bags and photographic equipment through blizzards, snow and ice, with the temperature in Norway falling as low as -17°C/ 1.4°F.

We would like to thank all the people who welcomed us into their beautiful wooden homes for their generosity and kindness – without you, this book wouldn't have been possible. Also, huge thanks to everyone at RPS – Cindy, Leslie, Annabel, Megan and Jess – for giving us the opportunity to publish another book, and for being so supportive and patient. Thank you yet again to Debi. This is our fifth book together and it's hard to put into words what you do. You are simply the best interiors photographer – hardworking, calm and such fun to be with.

To all at Baileys, thank you, especially Kirstin, Laura, Robyn and Emily. Finally, thanks to our family – Lucy, Ben and Cathryn and our mischievous grandchildren Fergus and Beau, for keeping us so amused.